I SURVIVED

TRUE STORIES

COURAGEOUS CREATURES

COURAGEOUS CREATURES

Lauren Tarshis

SCHOLASTIC INC.

For Dick Robinson

CONTENTS

AUTHOR'S NOTE

Hello Readers!

I'm so happy to be sharing the fourth I Survived True Stories book with you.

Like the first three, *Courageous Creatures* is different from the "main" books in my I Survived series. Those books are historical fiction novels. That means that all of the information is true—I do tons of research for each one. But the characters are fictional, inspired by real people, but brought to life from my imagination.

The four articles in this book are all works of nonfiction—they are true stories. But I hope you'll agree that the animals and people in each story are as unusual and inspiring as any characters from fiction. And their stories are every bit as exciting.

You'll meet a pigeon hero from World War I. You'll read about two dolphins that escaped death after being captured for a swim-with-the-dolphins program. You'll experience the biggest animal rescue in history, and travel to the wilds of Africa to meet two tough little cheetah cubs.

All of these stories started out as articles I wrote for *Storyworks*, a magazine that millions of kids read in their classrooms. I expanded each one, and then added lots of additional facts and information.

My hope is that these stories will spark your curiosity and inspire you to take action—to learn more on your own, to share information with your family and friends, to join the mission to make our world better for animals and humans. Maybe one day, I'll write a true story about you!

Happy reading adventures,

THE PIGEON HERO OF WORLD WAR I

The incredible true story of Cher Ami, the bird that saved nearly 200 American soldiers.

The American soldiers were doomed.

It was October 1918, not long before the end of World War I. This was a war more brutal than any before in history. Already millions were dead. More than 135 countries were losing soldiers in battles around the world.

Right now, in a dark, rainy forest in northeastern France, several hundred American troops were in a fight for their lives. The men were surrounded by enemy German soldiers.

Machine guns rattled. Bombs rained from the sky. The shouts and moans of wounded soldiers rose up. The Americans needed help. Their only hope was to get an urgent message to their commanders, 25 miles away.

But how? There were no walkie-talkies or cell phones in 1918, no computers to send emails, and the army radios weren't working.

Luckily, there was one brave warrior who had been trained for a moment exactly like this. She took off with the message, on a life-and-death race across the forest.

Her name was Cher Ami, and she was not a soldier. She was not even a human.

She was a pigeon.

INCREDIBLE POWERS

Cher Ami wasn't just any pigeon. Cher Ami (which means "dear friend" in French) was a special kind of bird—a carrier pigeon (sometimes called a homing pigeon). She was one of hundreds of carrier pigeons that helped the American military during World War I. Pigeons had an important job: to carry messages.

Why would the army use a pigeon to carry a message? For one thing, these pigeons are fast—some can fly up to 90 miles per hour.

They are also supersmart. A pigeon's brain is no bigger than a wad of bubble gum. But like the tiny chip in an iPhone, that pigeon brain is packed with power. For example, pigeons can be trained to

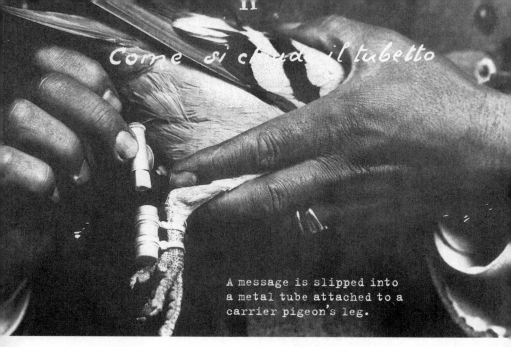

A message is slipped into a metal tube attached to a carrier pigeon's leg.

recognize letters and words.

But what truly makes these pigeons ideal for carrying messages is a unique talent. They always return to their home nest, no matter how far away it is. Nobody needs to show them how to get home. They just know. These humble gray birds can travel over oceans and mountains. They can fly across hundreds of twisting and turning miles. They can fly through thick fog and wild storms. And they almost never get lost.

It's this remarkable ability to navigate—to find their way—that makes them such incredible messengers.

But how does it actually work? How does the

CARRYING PIGEONS
A soldier brings carrier pigeons onto the battlefield.

MISERY ON THE BATTLEFIELDS
Soldiers wore masks to protect them from poison gas used by Germany.

IN THE TRENCHES
Soldiers spent weeks fighting from these muddy pits.

pigeon carry the message?

Imagine this. Say you wanted to use a carrier pigeon to carry *your* messages. First, you'd have to buy a carrier pigeon. You'd bring it home and create a nest for it at your house—on your roof, maybe, or in your yard.

Now imagine you are going to your friend's house. You would take the bird with you in a small cage. When you were ready for your parents to pick you up, you would write a message to them on a tiny piece of paper. You would roll the paper up and place it in a pinkie-sized metal tube attached to the pigeon's leg. You'd let your pigeon fly away. Its instinct would tell it to go to its home nest—back at your house.

Once it landed on its nest, a little bell would ring. This would signal to your parents that your pigeon was back. They would read the message—and head out to bring you home.

BRUTAL BATTLES

Of course, today it's much easier to just call or text your parents when you need something. Communicating is simple, even over long distances.

But until about 120 years ago, carrier pigeons like Cher Ami were actually the quickest way to send a message to someone who was very far away.

Ship captains used pigeons to send weather reports back to shore. Knights took pigeons with them into battle and used them to send news back to their kings. At the first Olympics, nearly three thousand years ago, pigeons carried the results of chariot races and gymnastics tournaments to surrounding cities.

In the 1800s, new inventions like the telegraph and the telephone transformed the way humans communicated. But in wartime, getting

World War I was the first time tanks were used on battlefields.

information across long distances was still difficult, especially during battles.

And in World War I, the battles were bigger and bloodier than the world had ever seen. New weapons unleashed terror and death on a massive scale. Machine guns fired hundreds of bullets a minute. Poison gas caused blistering burns and scorched lungs. Grenades injured or killed multiple people at close range. Tanks plowed across lines of

THE WORLD AT WAR
Soldiers from countries around the world fought in WWI battles. The biggest and deadliest battles happened in France.

WORLD WAR I FACT

More than 8 million soldiers died in battle and from diseases.

defense, and airplanes dropped bombs that triggered colossal explosions.

Modern technologies had made killing far too easy. But when it came to sending messages from a battlefield, no new invention was as reliable as a pigeon.

FEAR AND RATS

Cher Ami was born in England and trained by one of the country's most famous pigeon experts. She was brought to France to serve during World War I. Cher Ami's home nest was at the American army headquarters near the edge of a forest called Argonne.

In peacetime, Argonne was a fairy tale forest of towering trees and babbling brooks. But by the time Cher Ami arrived in France, World War I had been

WORLD WAR I FACT

At first, this war was often called "The Great War."

dragging on for four years. The forests and fields of France had been transformed into blood-soaked battlefields. These areas were haunted by the ghosts of hundreds of thousands of dead soldiers.

Most battles in World War I were fought with something called trench warfare. Trenches were deep, narrow ditches that stretched for miles. Most were about ten feet deep and five feet wide, and some stretched for dozens of miles.

Being in a trench meant that a soldier was partially protected from enemy gunfire. But eventually, it was time to push forward. During a battle, both sides would try to take over the other's trench.

Progress was slow—and bloody. Each time the men left their trench, they faced a storm of gunfire and bombs.

SICKENING STENCH

But men didn't just fight from the trenches. They lived in them—twenty-four hours a day, often for weeks at a time.

They coped with knee-deep mud, with the sickening stench of garbage and human waste, with disease, with constant fear.

And the noise—this is what soldiers would never forget. For days at a time, their ears would be pounded by the sounds of machine guns and bomb blasts.

Sleep was almost impossible. Soldiers who did manage to fall asleep often awoke to find rats scurrying across their chests.

Cher Ami joined the men of a large battalion of American soldiers that was part of the 77th Infantry Division. The man in charge, Major Charles Whittlesey, had been ordered to lead his

Major Charles Whittlesey

troops in an attack on the Germans in Argonne. Cher Ami was one of eight pigeons brought on the mission. The birds lived together in a cage, and their caretaker, a young soldier from New York, did his best to keep them safe as the troops moved through the forest.

UNDER ATTACK

Deep in the forest, on October 3, Whittlesey's men had accidentally marched into the path of a large German force. The Americans were soon surrounded and under fierce attack.

The men—there were about 550 of them—tried to fight back. But they were low on bullets. They were also badly outnumbered and exhausted. After all, many hadn't had much sleep for weeks. Food had run low. The only way for the men to get a sip of water while in the trenches was to risk crawling through the mud to a stream.

The Germans pummeled the American troops with artillery—blasting them with powerful explosives and grenades and rapid-fire machine guns. With each passing hour, more men were killed or wounded.

Whittlesey kept sending out pigeons carrying desperate requests for help. But one by one, the pigeons were shot or disappeared.

Finally, the next day, American planes appeared overhead. Whittlesey's men cheered, believing the planes would drop much-needed food, ammunition, and other supplies. But it wasn't food and bullets those planes were dropping.

TENDING THE WOUNDED
Soldiers trained in first aid were called medics.

It was bombs.

Whittlesey understood with horror that the Americans didn't realize that he and his men were in this part of the forest. The bombs were meant for the Germans, but instead, they were killing Whittlesey's men.

The major frantically scrawled a message announcing their location in the woods and that they were under American attack.

The message ended with a plea:

FOR HEAVEN'S SAKE, STOP IT.

PIGEON MESSAGE

RECEIVED AT MESSAGE CENTER 4:22 PM

TO C. O. 308th INFANTRY

FROM 1st BN 308th INFANTRY

WE ARE ALONG THE ROAD PARALELL 276.4. OUR ARTILLERY IS DROPPING A BARRAGE DIRECTLY ON US. FOR HEAVENS SAKE STOP IT.

WHITTLESAY
MAJ 308th

BIRD RELEASED 3 P.M.

RECEIVED AT LOFT 4:05 PM.
DISTRIBUTON
G 3
G 3 BULLETIN BOARD
C OF S
G 2
152 FIELD ARTILLERY BRIGADE
FILE

THE FAMOUS MESSAGE
The message Cher Ami carried saved nearly 200 lives.

A FEATHERED MISSILE

Cher Ami

By this time, only two pigeons were left: Cher Ami and one other. It was the other pigeon that was pulled from the cage first. But the bird was so terrified that it flapped away before the message could be placed into its tube.

Now it was up to Cher Ami.

Hands reached into the cage and gently lifted her out. When the message was secure, she was set free. She fluttered up to a tree branch and perched there, rock still. It was as though she needed a moment to gather her courage.

And then she took off, like a tiny, feathered missile.

The sky was a storm of bullets and shards of bomb-shattered trees. Almost immediately, a bullet hit her in the eye. She began falling toward the ground, bleeding. But Cher Ami didn't give up. She flapped her wings and rose skyward again.

Another bullet hit her, this time in her chest.

But she kept flying.

A third bullet struck her right leg and nearly tore it off.

But she kept flying.

MIRACULOUS JOURNEY

Twenty minutes after she'd taken off, Cher Ami—bloodied, half-blind, with her leg hanging by a thread—arrived at headquarters with her message. The bombing was halted and soldiers were sent to rescue Whittlesey and his embattled men.

Meanwhile, medics worked frantically to save Cher Ami's life. Her leg had to be amputated, but Cher Ami survived. She was fitted with a tiny wooden leg. News of her miraculous journey spread around the world. She was awarded a medal and sent to America, where she was greeted as a hero who had saved the lives of nearly two hundred men.

World War I ended five weeks after the last flight of Cher Ami. This terrible war caused death and suffering for people around the world. But in the midst of this misery emerged stories of great bravery and heroism. Like the story of Cher Ami, the courageous pigeon hero of World War I.

Cher Ami's body
was stuffed, and
is displayed at
the Smithsonian
National Museum
of American
History, in
Washington, D.C.

THE PIGEON HERO FILES

Turn the page to learn more about pigeons and other animal heroes.

IF YOU WERE A PIGEON...

There are 308 different kinds of pigeons, and they come in all different colors and sizes.

Cher Ami was a rock pigeon, similar to those you see in city parks.

Here's what your life would be like if you were a pigeon like Cher Ami.

You might live in a city...

Most pigeons around the world live in cities.

...Or you might live in the country.

You are very adaptable!

You'd also be called a dove. *Doves* and *pigeons* are different names for the same bird. Scientists would say you are a member of the Columbidae family.

24

You'd eat almost anything.

You prefer nuts and seeds, but you would often eat leftover human food.

I'm not picky!

You'd build your nest in a secret place.

In the wilderness, you'd find a cliff or ledge.
In the city, you'd choose a spot high on a building.

You'd take good care of your babies.

Moms and dads take turns caring for their chicks.

You wouldn't live long.

Just about 2½ years.

You'd have some VERY fancy cousins.

These are Jacobin pigeons, one of dozens of your beautiful pigeon relatives.

HOW DO PIGEONS FIND THEIR WAY HOME?

Scientists aren't exactly sure, but they have some theories.

1 They use their eyes

Homing pigeons may use the position and angle of the sun, plus trees, mountains, and other natural landmarks, to help them keep track of where they are and where they want to go. They may also use human-made landmarks, like buildings and bridges.

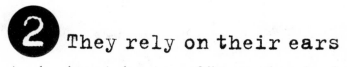

② They rely on their ears

Another theory is that pigeons follow sounds too low for humans to hear. These sounds are called *infrasound*, and are created by Earth itself—from the crust beneath the surface of the Earth, the oceans, even weather patterns.

Every place has unique infrasounds. **Think of it this way:** If you closed your eyes and just listened, you'd be able to tell if you were in your school gym rather than your bedroom at home.

③ They use Earth's magnetic field

This is called *magnetoreception*. Researchers have even suggested that pigeons have special powers within their beaks—tiny specks of iron that act like compasses.

Sniff
Sniff

④ They follow their nose

Finally, some researchers think homing pigeons may use their sense of smell to guide them.

ANIMAL SUPER NAVIGATORS

Here are some other animals that have amazing powers to find their way home.

Bees

Some types of bees can find their way home from as far away as eight miles. Honeybees can even communicate directions to their food sources to other honeybees through a special dance.

Wild salmon

Salmon are born in freshwater streams and migrate to the ocean. When it is time for them to lay their eggs years later, adult salmon swim thousands of miles back to the same stream where they were born. Scientists believe salmon rely on both their sense of smell and Earth's magnetic field to guide them.

Monarch butterflies

In the summer, the eastern North American monarch butterfly makes its home in the northeastern United States and southern Canada. But every October, these butterflies flutter up to 2,000 miles south to the mountains of central Mexico. They stay there until spring. Since monarch butterflies have a very short life, the butterflies that arrive in Mexico each year have never been there before. Scientists believe the migrating monarchs use the position of the sun to find their way.

Ants

Ants can scurry back to their nests even after they have been moved to a new location they've never been to before. They use their powerful eyes to get home. This is known as "visual homing."

European eels

European eels lay eggs in the Sargasso Sea, then the babies travel thousands of miles to rivers across Europe. And then they return to the Sargasso Sea where they were born.

WHEN PIGEONS DELIVERED MAIL

How a tragic shipwreck turned pigeons into mail carriers.

IN 1894, there was a tragic shipwreck off the coast of New Zealand. More than 135 people died. Survivors came ashore to an island called Great Barrier Island, 60 miles from the main island of New Zealand.

At the time, Great Barrier Island was almost completely cut off from New Zealand and the rest of the world. Mail and messages came only once a week, by ship. That's why news of the tragic shipwreck—and of those who survived— took three days to get to New Zealand.

Left: The wreck
of the *Wairarapa*.

Above: Each pigeon
could carry up to six
letters, which were
written on tissue-thin
paper, rolled up, and
placed in tubes.

Right: A rare
pigeon-gram stamp.

This tragedy made it clear that New Zealand needed a better way to send important messages to and from the Great Barrier Island. And this is how, two years later, the world's first "pigeon post" was born. Carrier pigeons carried messages to and from Great Barrier Island in just 90 minutes.

The pigeon mail service lasted only about ten years; new technology like telegraphs and telephones replaced the pigeons.

But today the rare surviving "pigeon-gram" stamps are prized by collectors and worth thousands of dollars each.

MEET STUBBY

THE DOG HERO OF WORLD WAR I

This dashing terrier is named Stubby. Like Cher Ami, he was an animal hero of World War I. He became world-famous for helping American soldiers in France.

He cheered up wounded men. He kept the troops safe by sniffing out poisonous gas, and even helped catch a German spy!

Stubby was wounded more than once and even wore a special gas mask to protect him in combat.

When the Germans were defeated in 1918, Stubby returned to the United States a hero. He marched in parades, appeared in newspaper articles, and met three presidents.

When he died in 1926, Stubby was mourned by millions of people across the country.

Animals in Wartime

From carrying soldiers to sniffing out bombs, animals have had many jobs in wartime.

Horses

Greek warriors and medieval knights rode into battle on horseback. Horses continued to join soldiers on battlefields through World War I, when they were replaced by jeeps, trucks and tanks.

Glowworms

During World War I, soldiers captured these glowing beetles and used the them as mini-lights for reading in the trenches.

Cats

Humans have long relied on cats to catch mice and rats. These rodents spread disease and destroy food supplies. During World War I and World War II, cats were brought onto ships and into trenches.

Dogs

In today's military, dogs are prized for their sense of smell. They are often used to sniff for explosives and to find survivors of bombings.

HONORING BATTLEFIELD ANIMALS

Throughout history, humans have relied on animals—especially pigeons, horses, and dogs—for help on battlefields. Here are some ways that people have honored these war-hero animals.

Australia

The War Dog Memorial, in the city of Canberra.

England

Animals in War Memorial, in London's Hyde Park.

The monument
to carrier
pigeons,
in Lille,
France.

SHOULD CHER AMI BE BURIED IN A HERO'S CEMETERY?

After Cher Ami died in 1919, her body was stuffed. Today, she is on display in Washington, D.C., at the Smithsonian Museum of American History. But some feel she should be buried in a U.S. military cemetery along with other soldiers who died from wartime injuries.

What do you think?

Arlington
National
Cemetery,
outside
Washington,
D.C., is the
largest
military
cemetery
in the U.S.

THE DOLPHIN DEFENDER

Two dolphins were near death. He helped save them, and thousands more.

Two dolphins were in trouble.

That's what filmmaker Hardy Jones learned one morning in 2004. A man called him from the small Central American country of Nicaragua. He gave Jones terrible news: Two dolphins had been captured in the Caribbean Sea, 20 miles off the coast of Nicaragua.

The men who caught them had been hoping to sell them to a resort hotel with a swim-with-the-dolphins program (SWTD). There are thousands of these programs around the world. Vacationers pay for the chance to climb into a pool or lagoon, and splash and play with live dolphins. Hotel owners will pay thousands of dollars for captured dolphins. But in this case, a sale didn't happen.

And so the men who had captured the dolphins left them to die in a filthy tank.

Jones, who had devoted most of his life to helping ocean creatures, leaped into action.

"I was on a plane as fast as I could move," Jones said.

By the time Jones arrived in Nicaragua, the two dolphins—he would soon name them Nica and Blue Fields—had been trapped for two weeks. The government of Nicaragua had already called in a rescue team from the World Society for the Protection of Animals (WSPA) to help. The dolphins were in desperate condition—weak, starving, and terrified. The scientists from WSPA worked to help the dolphins. They fed them fish filled with nutrients. They comforted them as best they could, patting them gently and speaking in gentle voices.

But this was a crisis. It was clear to everyone that the dolphins would not survive even a few days more in the toxic pool.

DOLPHIN FACT

In the wild, dolphins live in groups with their families and friends.

The only hope was a daring mission, one that put the dolphins at great risk. WSPA scientists, along with soldiers from the Nicaraguan military, would try to get the dolphins home. They would attempt to return them to the spot in the Caribbean Sea where they had been captured. The extraordinary journey would require two boats and a helicopter.

Jones would have an important role on this mission: filming it. This was part of his goal to help ocean creatures. Over the years, Jones created many films that showed how human greed and carelessness threatened dolphins, one of Earth's most intelligent and sensitive creatures. His films have helped save the lives of millions of dolphins, earning him a nickname worthy of a superhero: the Dolphin Defender.

"HE'S CRYING"

Jones's camera was running as Nica and Blue Fields were carefully hoisted out of the water on slings. It took four men to carry each of the more than 300-pound animals to a waiting boat. The dolphins were placed on padded trays. The team slathered them with cream to protect them from the glaring sun and cooled them with seawater to prevent them from overheating.

Nica closed her eyes and seemed to surrender to whatever awaited her. Blue Fields made quiet, high-pitched whistling noises.

"He's crying," Jones said softly.

Nobody knew if the dolphins would survive the journey. Whatever happened to them, though, Jones would make sure that the world knew their story.

WILDLIFE WARRIOR
A young Hardy Jones tends to a small whale captured in Japan. He eventually helped free this and other whales. During his life, Jones helped save the lives of thousands of sea mammals.

AN EXTRAORDINARY BOND

In the late 1970s, when Jones began making films, little was known about dolphins in the wild. Jones was a passionate scuba diver and had long dreamed of swimming with dolphins at sea in their natural environment. But experts said it could not be done. They told Jones that if he got too close, the dolphins would flee or perhaps turn violent.

But Jones had heard about a pod—an extended family—of friendly spotted dolphins often seen at a particular site about 70 miles off the coast of Florida. A treasure hunter helped him find these dolphins. From the moment Jones entered the water, he was welcomed into their midst.

In fact, the dolphins seemed as curious about Jones as he was about them. They swam up to him, studying him closely. When he removed his T-shirt and let it float in the water, a dolphin grabbed it and swam away. Moments later, the dolphin reappeared and dropped the shirt in front of Jones. "It was clear to me that he knew the shirt belonged to me," Jones recalled.

Jones was amazed by the animals' intelligence and the closeness of the group. The dolphins doted on one another, cuddling close together and stroking each other with their fins. Mothers

ALWAYS TOGETHER
Dolphins travel in groups called "pods" that include members of their families.

lavished attention on their young. The animals seemed to communicate with each other constantly, in a language of clicks, whistles, and high-pitched shrieks that vibrated through the water.

Jones would later realize that humans should not try to interact closely with dolphins or other sea creatures. But those early experiences helped Jones form an extraordinary bond with dolphins. It wasn't long before he decided to leave his work in television to devote himself full time to protecting them and other creatures of the sea.

6 MILLION DEAD

When Jones started his work, tens of thousands of dolphins were dying every year. The biggest problem was the tuna industry. In the ocean, tuna tend to swim beneath dolphins, so the nets used by tuna boats entangled dolphins. The dolphins, which must surface to breathe every ten minutes, suffocated. Some tuna boats killed hundreds of dolphins during each trip; since the late 1950s, tuna fishing has killed more than six million dolphins.

Even more brutal were the dolphin hunts taking place in Japan, which has a long tradition of hunting and eating dolphins. Fishermen would

DOLPHINS IN DANGER
Above: A dolphin hunt
in western Japan.
Below: A dolphin caught
in a fishing net.

More than half of all dolphins captured in the wild die within three months.

drive pods of dolphins close to the shore and trap them. The youngest and best-looking dolphins were separated, loaded onto boats, and shipped off to aquariums to perform for humans. The rest were slaughtered for their meat, or killed so they wouldn't compete with the fishermen for fish.

News of these hunts led Jones to travel to Japan, where he captured horrifying scenes of slaughter on film. The memory of these scenes caused Jones's voice to shake with anger and sadness even years later.

The film he took of these hunts was shown on television around the world, sparking outrage and protests. Many of the villages reduced or even eliminated their hunts, and thousands of dolphins were undoubtedly spared.

"It was the first time I realized just how powerful a man with a camera could be," Jones said.

In the coming years, Jones would make more films. One, about dolphins dying in the tuna nets, led to massive protests against tuna companies like StarKist and Bumble Bee. Tens of thousands of people saw the film and stopped buying tuna. They wrote furious letters to the companies' leaders and demanded that more be done to protect dolphins. This public outcry led American tuna companies to change their fishing practices. Today, almost all tuna sold by American companies is "dolphin safe."

100 MILES A DAY

Dolphins continue to face serious threats, however. They are endangered by ocean pollution, climate change, overfishing, and continued hunting in parts of Asia, Africa, and South America. (It is illegal to hunt or capture dolphins in U.S. waters.) But in recent years, a fast-growing threat is the capture of wild dolphins, like Nica and Blue Fields, for dolphin shows and swim-with-the-dolphins programs at resorts and hotels, and on cruise ships.

"Get up close and personal with the amazing bottlenose dolphins!" says a website for one SWTD program in Florida. A photograph shows a man

FUN OR CRUEL?

Dozens of resorts and hotels around the world allow guests to swim in pools and lagoons with dolphins.

Many guests have no idea that these programs are harmful to dolphins and could be dangerous for the human swimmers, too.

clinging to the fins of two dolphins while they pull him through the water. The man is grinning with excitement. And, it appears, so are the dolphins.

SOCIAL CREATURES

But such images can lie. Dolphins don't smile to express joy as humans do. Their mouths are naturally upturned; even a dolphin lying dead wears the same "smiling" expression of a dolphin carrying a tourist on its back.

It's true that some aquariums provide loving care for their captive dolphins. But in the wild, dolphins swim up to 100 miles in a single day. They form close family relationships, like humans do, and friendships that can last for decades. It's hard to imagine that such a free-roaming and social creature could ever be content in a concrete-and-Plexiglas pen. Indeed, 53 percent of wild dolphins die within three months of being captured.

Nica and Blue Fields were spared that fate, thanks to the extraordinary efforts of the WSPA and the Nicaraguan government. The dolphins had survived the first boat ride and a helicopter trip. Now they were on another boat, speeding across the Caribbean Sea.

The boat stopped near the place where the dolphins had been captured. Jones's camera was running as the team released the dolphins off the side of the boat.

Nica went first. The moment she hit the water,

The slaughter of dolphins continues in Japan despite protests from people in Japan and around the world.

she took off. When Blue Fields hit the water, he seemed confused, as though he had just woken up from a nightmare. At last, he swam off. Hopefully, they would find their family. Bottlenose dolphins can live as long as sixty years in the wild. We can only hope that Nica and Blue Fields are still alive today, swimming free in the Caribbean Sea.

But, of course we can't know for sure.

Hardy Jones died in 2018, but his mission continues.

Thanks to Jones, though, the world will not forget the story of Nica and Blue Fields. The film footage he shot of their ordeal was seen by millions of people. In the years after, he continued his mission to protect dolphins and other sea creatures. He died in 2018, at the age of 75, and will always be remembered for his extraordinary work.

Through his films, he showed that humans can threaten dazzling animals like dolphins.

But he is also an example to us all of how we can help animals, too.

THE
DOLPHIN
FILES

Turn the page to find out more about
dolphins and other fascinating creatures
of the sea.

There are more than 40 different species of dolphins. Nica and Blue Fields are bottlenose dolphins, the most common kind.

IF YOU WERE A BOTTLENOSE DOLPHIN...

You would be fast, one of the fastest swimmers in the ocean, reaching speeds of 18 miles an hour. You might swim as far as 100 miles in a single day.

You would be very noisy. You would communicate with other dolphins in a language of clicks, squeaks, moans, barks, groans, yelps, and whistles.

Groan
Yelp
Squeak

You wouldn't be alone. Dolphins live together in groups known as "pods" with twenty or thirty dolphins—or hundreds. Your pod would include your family and friends.

Click
Click
Click

You would live in any ocean that isn't freezing cold.

You would eat fish, shrimp, squid, and crabs. You would grab your meal with your small, cone-shaped teeth. But you wouldn't chew. Dolphins swallow food whole. *Gulp!*

You would have a "whistle name." Dolphin mothers actually name their babies using a unique whistle sound.

You would not be able to breathe underwater, but you could hold your breath for as long as twelve minutes.

You would watch out for sharks, which are the only sea creatures big enough to hunt and eat you.

You would live to be 40 to 60 years old, and could grow to be 13 feet long.

Who, me?

DOLPHINS' SUPERPOWER ECHO

Imagine you are swimming in the deep, dark, noisy ocean. You're hungry and want to track down a juicy fish to eat. How do you find it? If you were a dolphin, you would use sound waves. This amazing power is called echolocation.

Bats also use echolocation.

Echolocation lets me "see" in the pitch dark.

LOCATION

HOW ECHOLOCATION WORKS

 Dolphins make whistling and clicking sounds using "lips" on top of their heads.

 These sounds create invisible waves in the ocean (known as sound waves).

 The sound waves bounce off other animals or objects, and come back to the dolphins as echoes.

 Dolphins "hear" the echoes in special parts of their bodies located on their lower jaws and foreheads.

 The echoes let them figure out the size and shape of the object or animal. They can even tell how fast and in which direction a moving animal is traveling!

AMAZING FACTS

DOLPHINS ARE STAR ATHLETES.

Spinner dolphins can leap up to 14 times in a row. Striped dolphins can also do somersaults, tail spins, and backward flips.

DOLPHINS SLEEP WITH ONE EYE OPEN.

Scientists aren't exactly sure why. But they believe it's so they can watch out for predators and make sure their family and friends are close.

DOLPHINS HAVE TWO STOMACHS.

One stores the food and the other digests it.

ABOUT DOLPHINS

DOLPHINS ARE SUPERSMART.

Scientists believe they are more intelligent than dogs, whales, walruses, seals, and porpoises.

> Hey! I'm a genius!

DOLPHINS ARE NOT FISH.

They look like fish. They swim like fish. But they are mammals because . . .

- Dolphins breathe air.
- Dolphins *don't* lay eggs— mammal babies are born alive.
- Dolphin babies can drink milk from their mothers.
- Dolphins are warm-blooded.

> We are fish because we are cold-blooded and breathe underwater using our gills.

Turn the page to learn more about marine mammals.

THE WORLD OF MARINE MAMMALS

1 Cetaceans [si-TAY-shuns]

Whales, dolphins, and porpoises
They look like fish and spend their whole lives in the water. But like all marine mammals, they must come to the surface to breathe.

I look like a dolphin, but I'm a porpoise. Check out my rounder nose and fin—that's how you can tell us apart.

This humpback whale is one of 7 kinds of whales known as baleen whales. They don't have teeth. Instead, they eat by swimming with their mouths open and skimming plants and fish from the water as they move.

The blue whale is the biggest creature on Earth. It is 100 feet long—as long as two school buses.

Dolphins are one of 48 different kinds of mammals that depend on the sea for their survival.

② Pinnipeds [PIN-I-peds]

Seals, walruses, and sea lions
These "flipper footed" animals live mostly in the water but come onto land to raise their young and to rest.

There are 32 different kinds of seals that live along beaches in many parts of the world with cold water. But most live in the Arctic.

Leopard seals are feared predators of the Arctic.

All walrus live in the Arctic, but there are 2 main types: Atlantic and Pacific. Both males and females have tusks.

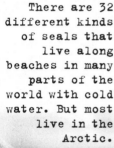

I weigh about 1.5 tons—as much as a car.

③ Sirenians [si-REE-NEE-ins]

Manatees and dugongs

These gentle, slow-moving creatures are also called sea cows.
They look so much alike they can be hard to tell apart.

Manatees have good eyesight and can live in both fresh water and salt water. They live only about half as long as dugongs.

Dungongs live in salt water, and live to be 70 years old. They have very poor eyesight and rely on their noses to find food.

Centuries ago, sailors who saw sea cows believed they were seeing mermaids.

④ Fissipeds *[FIS-i-peds]*

Polar bears and sea otters

Pandas, dogs, and raccoons are also fissipeds. What do they all have in common? Their paws have toes.

But like other sea mammals, otters and polar bears depend on the ocean for their food.

Sea otters live along the coasts of North America and Asia. They spend most of their lives in the water. They even sleep in the water!

Polar bears live on ice floes in the Arctic. If they have to, they can swim for days to find their food. Their favorite prey is seals, but they also eat birds and fish.

Under our white fur, our skin is black.

POLAR BEAR FACT They have a powerful sense of smell and can sniff out a seal from 20 miles away.

Thank you for helping protect me!

BE A DOLPHIN DEFENDER!

Simple ways to help marine mammals and protect our oceans and rivers.

① Don't Use Plastic

Plastic straws, water bottles, and bags often end up in the oceans, where they harm sea creatures. Plastic pollution kills at least 100,000 sea mammals every year, including species that are endangered. Plastic also kills more than one million sea birds.

Use paper straws, reusable bags, and reusable water bottles instead of plastic. And convince your friends to ditch plastic, too.

Turtles often eat plastic bags thinking they're jellyfish.

② Eat the Right Seafood

Eating seafood can be healthy and delicious. But certain kinds of fish are disappearing from oceans and shouldn't be on restaurant menus, at markets—or our plates.

Also, some big fishing companies use football-field-sized nets that also kill sea mammals like dolphins and whales. We should avoid eating fish caught in this harmful way, and support fishing companies that catch and sell fish responsibly.

How can you get information to help you make good choices?

Go to **Seafoodwatch.org**; it has all the information you and your family need to make good choices.

③ Don't Swim With Dolphins

As you learned in the story of Nica and Blue Fields, swim-with-the-dolphins programs are cruel to dolphins. Share this information with your family and friends. Dolphins and other sea mammals belong free in the sea, not captive for our entertainment.

④ Learn All You Can

The more you know about dolphins and oceans, the more inspired you will be to work to protect them. Maybe you will be the next Hardy Jones!

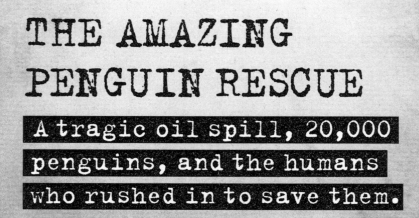

THE AMAZING PENGUIN RESCUE

A tragic oil spill, 20,000 penguins, and the humans who rushed in to save them.

Imagine you are an African penguin living on an island in the South Atlantic Ocean. You are a large black-and-white bird, almost two feet tall.

You live with tens of thousands of other penguins on a rocky beach. There used to be millions and millions of you, living on islands like this one, scattered off the western and southern coasts of Africa.

Now there are only about 41,000 of you left in the world. Like many other species of penguins, you are endangered—but you don't know this.

Because remember, you are a penguin. And on this cold and windy day in June of 2000, you are living happily on your rocky beach with thousands of other penguins.

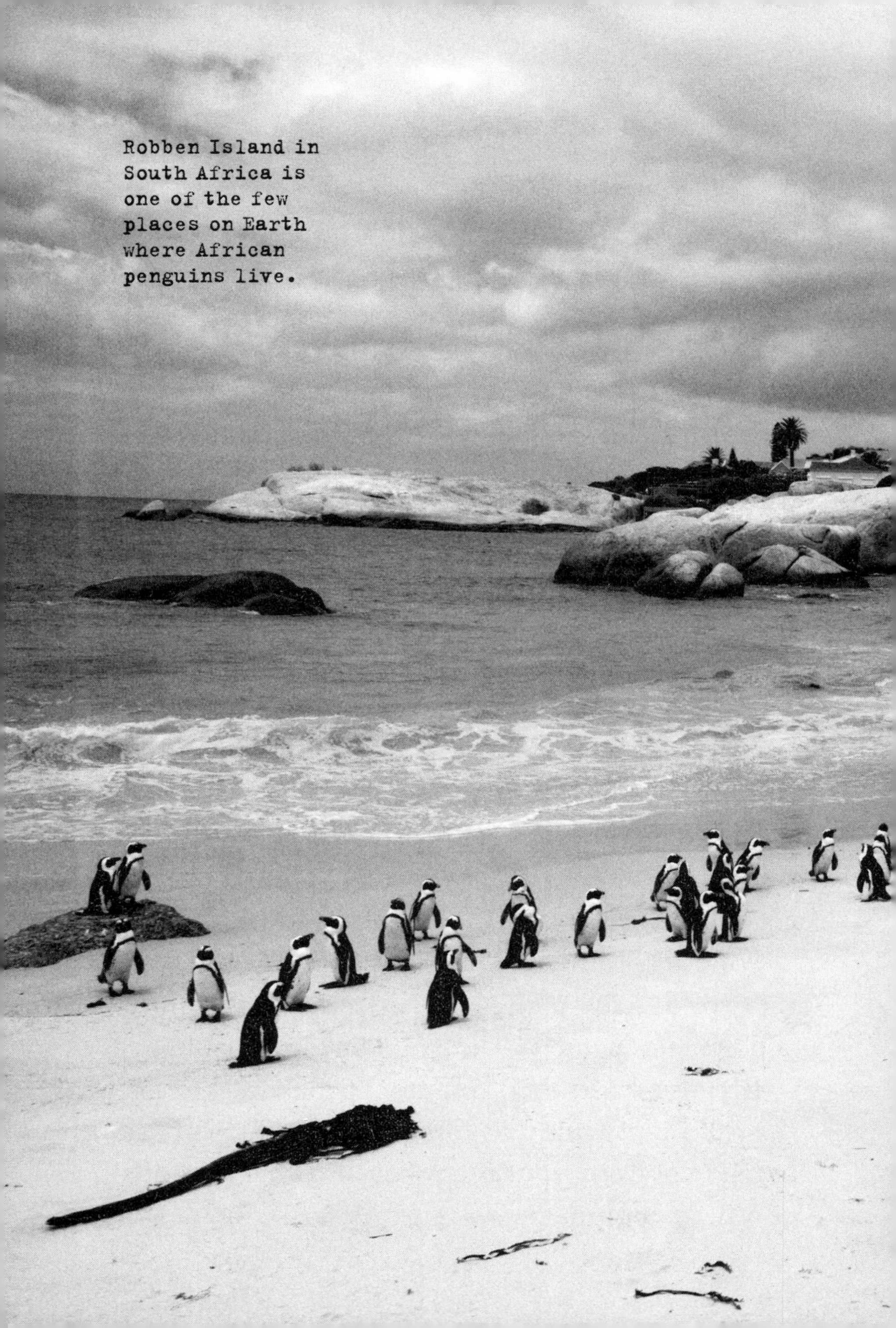

Robben Island in
South Africa is
one of the few
places on Earth
where African
penguins live.

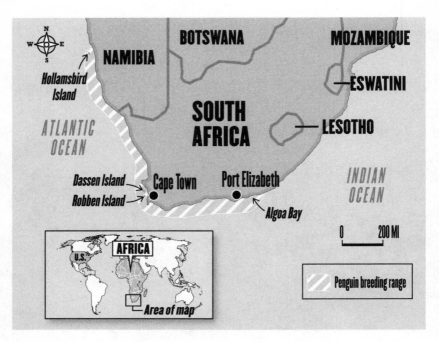

The beach echoes with penguin noises: barks and honks. Some of your fellow penguins fight for territory, while others cuddle with their mates or care for their fluffy little chicks.

Your tiny stomach rumbles—it's time to find your next meal. So you head down the rocky beach to the water's edge. You waddle on your tiny feet.

Your little wings are too stubby for flying—no penguins can fly. But who needs to fly when you're an African penguin?

You can swim faster and dive deeper than almost any other bird on Earth. As you plunge into the sea, your wings become powerful propellers. You

African penguins spend 75 percent of their time in the water.

shoot through the water at nearly 10 miles an hour, a black-and-white blur. You snatch sardines from the surface with your sharp beak. You don't have teeth, but you don't need them. You just gulp each of the wriggling little fish down whole.

The water is freezing cold. But you barely feel the chill. Your tightly packed feathers protect you.

You stay in the sea for hours, until your belly is full. And then you're ready to head back to shore.

That's when something goes wrong.

As you come to the surface for air, the water feels strange. It is too thick; it burns your eyes. You try to swim away, but suddenly your wings have become too heavy to lift. Your body wobbles and rolls. Wait. Why do you feel so cold? You shiver and gasp for breath. What is happening to you?

OIL SPILL DISASTER

What you do not know is that a few hours ago, a cargo ship called the *Treasure* suffered serious damage in the rough winter seas. The ship split apart. As it sank, 1,300 tons of toxic oil gushed into the ocean.

Now that oil surrounds your breeding ground—the largest African penguin breeding ground in the

world. You and thousands of other penguins have been trapped in the massive oil slick and are soaked with poisonous oil.

The impact of oil on a penguin (or any bird) is immediate and devastating. You are shivering because the oil has caused your feathers to clump and separate.

Normally, your feathers create a thick covering that protects you from the cold. You spend hours a day tending to your feathers—smoothing them with your beak. This is known as preening.

Your body even creates a special oil just for your feathers. Drops of this feather oil ooze from a little

An oil tanker crosses the ocean.

A penguin
coated
with oil.

opening near your tail. You coat your beak with this special oil and spread it over your feathers. Your mate helps you by smoothing the oil over your back and head. This is what makes your feathers waterproof.

But the toxic oil in the water destroyed this natural coating. Your feathers now clump together. This lets the freezing water lash at your sensitive skin. Your eyes hurt because the oil has burned them. Your wings are heavy because they are coated with oil and waterlogged.

PENGUIN FACT

Penguins live in some of the coldest and harshest places on Earth.

But your instinct for survival is strong, and somehow you struggle back to shore, fighting against the current. The journey, usually effortless, is an agonizing ordeal. You manage to stagger onto the beach and back to your nest, where you lick and peck at your feathers, desperate to clean them. Finally, you give up. There is nothing to do but stand there, terrified, dazed, silent.

SAVING YOUR LIFE

Then the beach is invaded by enormous creatures.

They are humans, but you don't know that. You have never seen a human before. These men and women understand what you don't: that this oil spill is a catastrophe for you and your species. Some of these people have dedicated their lives to helping birds like you, birds threatened by oil spills and other human-made disasters. They have participated in bird rescues around the world. All they care about is saving your life.

But how could you know this?

As these humans swarm the beach, you are overcome with panic. When a man catches you, you viciously fight him off. You don't have teeth. But your jaw is powerful. Your beak is razor sharp. You bite the man's arm, ripping his skin through the fabric of his thick coat. He doesn't let go, so you strike again, biting his leg and inflicting a wound that will leave a scar for the rest of his life. But he doesn't care about cuts or scars. At that moment, he just wants to help you.

Volunteers worked for days to care for the penguins.

PAINFUL WORK

All across the beach, dozens of people are capturing penguins. They are wincing as beaks tear their skin and wings slap them. They struggle to load terrified, oil-soaked birds into wooden crates. It is painful, exhausting work. The sight of all the scared and injured penguins is heartbreaking to the humans. Some fight back tears.

But they don't give up. Tens of thousands of penguins are facing death because of the oil spill. And these people are determined to save every single one.

Ten miles from the island, outside the city of Cape Town, a team of scientists and volunteers has transformed a warehouse into a penguin rescue center. They work with astonishing speed. The warehouse contains hundreds of round enclosures, each large enough to accommodate 100 penguins. Other areas of the warehouse have been designated for washing penguins. One room is filled with

Penguin food:
Sardines

10 tons of frozen fish, the amount needed daily to feed the penguins. Acquiring this enormous quantity of fish every day will be among the workers' great challenges.

SICKENING STINK

Actually, everything is a challenge. Simply getting one penguin to eat is almost impossible. In the wild, penguins hunt for sardines, gobbling them up while the fish are still alive and wriggling. These penguins won't accept dead fish from human hands, so they must be force-fed. To force-feed a penguin, a worker must restrain it, pry its beak open, and shove fish down its throat. Feeding one penguin can take an hour. Feeding all the penguins takes an army of workers fifteen hours.

And then there is the smell. The combined stench of penguin droppings, dead sardines, and human sweat fills the huge warehouse. The stink is so sickening that many people vomit when they first arrive.

As news of the rescue effort spreads, thousands of volunteers flock to the warehouse, eager to help. They are a diverse group, including wealthy women from fancy neighborhoods and poor teenagers from the streets of Cape Town. Some volunteers have experience rescuing wildlife; others have never owned a pet. All have one thing in common: a mission to save as many penguins as possible.

HELPING YOU RECOVER

For you, one of thousands of oil-soaked penguins, every hour brings new terrors. You are force-fed. Ointment is smeared onto your eyes to help heal them from the burning oil. A tube is stuck down your throat. This is so a medicine called liquid charcoal can be pumped down into your stomach.

At first you are in a swirl of pain and fear. But as the days go by, you begin to feel better. The ointment heals your eyes, and the liquid charcoal helps your body rid itself of the oil you swallowed. Those fish jammed down your throat give you strength.

And those strange creatures—the humans. They stop seeming so strange and scary. You no longer want to bite them or slap them with your wings. You open your mouth when they offer you fish. There is one woman who comes every day. You recognize her voice and greet her with one of your donkey-like honks.

Each penguin was carefully cleaned by hand.

GENTLE HANDS

After many weeks, it is, at last, your turn to be cleaned. You are taken to a room and placed into a plastic tub. A woman pours vegetable oil over you to loosen the caked-on oil. She washes you with mild soap and warm water, her gentle hands scrubbing your body inch by inch. She carefully cleans your eyes and ears with a toothbrush. You do not bite her. The next day, after your feathers are clean and dry, this woman picks you up and holds you close to her chest. You do not try to get away.

NEARLY 20,000 SAVED

One day, after several weeks have gone by, you are put into a box. You feel yourself being moved. When the box is opened, you are on an unfamiliar beach. You stand there until your instinct takes over; then you run to the water and plunge in. Soon you are on the shores of a rocky island.

Your island.

While you were gone, humans cleaned up the oil that had covered the beach. The ocean carried the rest away.

Before long, thousands of other penguins arrive on the island. The air is filled once again with honks and barks. You have no idea that you have

Volunteers watch and cheer as rescued penguins return home to the sea.

been part of the greatest animal rescue in history. Nearly 20,000 penguins were saved. In the coming weeks, researchers will be overjoyed to observe that many of the rescued birds are paired up with mates and sitting on eggs.

You don't think about any of this, because you are a penguin. All you know is that your world is finally as it should be.

THE PENGUIN FILES

Turn the page to learn more about African penguins and other species of these unique birds.

IF YOU WERE AN AFRICAN PENGUIN...

You would start life as an egg that your mother laid and kept safe in a hole in the ground.

You would be a small ball of fluff when you hatched from your egg. Your mom and dad would take turns feeding you and keeping you warm.

You would grow quickly, and within a few months you would be about 2 feet tall.

I'm one of the smaller penguin species.

Your favorite foods would be small fish like sardines and anchovies, as well as squid and shellfish.

You would watch out for predators both on the land and at sea—leopards; dogs; wild cats; sharks; seals; and orcas, a kind of dolphin also known as a killer whale.

HONK!

When you felt threatened, you would puff up your chest, hold back your wings, and thrust your beak forward, bobbing your head from side to side.

You would live for about 20 years.

You would be loud and make many different noises, including a honk that sounds like the bray of a donkey.

AMAZING
PENGUINS

They come in all shapes, sizes, and personalities. Here's a closer look at a few species of this astounding bird.

BIGGEST

Emperor penguin Emperor penguins can grow to be between three and four feet tall (that's the size of a kindergartner). They live in Antarctica and spend most of their time on floating ice.

TINIEST

Little penguin is also known as fairy penguin. The Maori people call them "karora." These cuties are only 13 inches tall. They live in southern Australia and New Zealand.

TOUGHEST

Adélie penguin [Ah-DELL-ee]
The adorable Adélie penguins of Antarctica are fearless, loud, and at times aggressive. They will attack much larger animals.

LOUDEST

When you're a macaroni penguin, every day is Crazy Hair Day!

Macaroni penguin
All penguins are noisy. But these critters are the loudest. They're also famous for their crowns, or "crest," of yellow feathers.

Gentoo penguin
All penguins are strong, fast swimmers. But gentoo is the speediest. They shoot through the water at 22 miles per hour, faster than the fastest human swimmer.

PENGUIN SUPERPOWERS

SWIMMING

Penguins can't fly. They are clumsy on land. But in the water, they are superstar swimmers. Their wings act like fins. Their strong, webbed feet are flippers that help them shoot through the water.

Humboldt penguins are one of the most powerful "poop bombers" of the penguin world.

POOPING!

Penguins have the amazing ability to shoot their poop 4 feet!

But they don't do it for fun. They do it because it lets them keep their dirty, stinky poop away from their nests.

MOLTING

Every year, a penguin loses every single one of its feathers, and then grows new ones. This process is called molting.

During the time the penguin is waiting for new feathers, it can't go into the water because it will freeze. So in the weeks before they molt, they stuff themselves with food.

Molting is miserable!

A king penguin as his new feathers grow in.

BIRDS THAT CAN'T FLY

Penguins are known as "flightless birds," and they're not alone. There are fifty other species of flightless birds—also called ratites—around the world. New Zealand has the most.

Penguins, ostriches, emus, and other ratites have wings that are too weak and stubby to lift them off the ground. They also don't have the strong chest bones and muscles that enable other birds to take flight.

These creatures are all related to creatures that did fly . . . hundreds of thousands or millions of years ago. But over time, they lost their flying ability. Why? Because they didn't need to fly to escape from predators or to find food.

ARE CHICKENS FLIGHTLESS?

NO! I can't fly far, but I can get myself off the ground for a few seconds.

OSTRICHES

can run faster than almost any other land animal—45 miles an hour. If an ostrich had raced your school bus, the ostrich probably would have won.

My wings can't lift me up, but they help me balance.

I have two eyelids—one for blinking, one to keep dirt from my eyes.

EMUS are also superfast, and almost as tall as ostriches.

THE WORLD OF

Arctic Ocean

Europe

North America

Atlantic Ocean

Africa

Pacific Ocean

South America

Atlantic Ocean

African Penguin

Gentoo Penguin

Humboldt Penguin

Southern Ocean

Antarctica

Southern Rockhopper Penguin

King Penguin

Adélie Penguin

PENGUINS

Penguins in the wild can be found mostly in the world's coldest spots, such as Antarctica. But some species live in warmer areas. Here's a quick look at where penguins live, and a few of the different species that can be found there.

Asia

Pacific Ocean

Indian Ocean

Australia

Little Penguin

Emperor Penguin

PENGUINS AT RISK

Penguins are at risk almost everywhere they live. Many species, like the African penguin, are endangered.

Main threats are climate change, oil spills, ocean pollution, and destruction of their habitats by humans.

FIRE ON THE OCEAN

THE BIGGEST OIL SPILL IN HISTORY

Every year, oil spills at sea cause harm to wildlife and our oceans. Most oil spills happen when big ships carrying oil become damaged during a voyage; this is what caused the oil spill that led to the great penguin rescue.

But the biggest oil spill in history, known as the Deepwater Horizon Oil Spill, happened on an oil rig. Oil rigs are huge platforms built over the ocean so that oil can be drilled from wells underneath the ocean floor.

The people who owned and ran the well didn't follow important safety rules. On April 20, 2010, disaster struck. A massive explosion and fire killed eleven workers and injured seventeen others.

More than 134 million gallons of oil gushed into the Gulf of Mexico. It spread for hundreds of miles, causing devastation to wildlife.

Thousands of sea mammals and birds were killed.

Oil washed up on beaches. Fishermen couldn't go to work.

Outrage over the Deepwater Horizon spill led to stricter safety rules.

But oil spills at sea and on land still threaten wildlife, the environment, and the health of people.

THE CHEETAH DADDY

When two cheetahs lost their mother, someone had to teach them to survive in the wild.

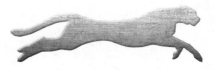

Deep in the wilderness of northern Kenya, two cheetah cubs lay huddled together under a bush. Their mother had hidden them before going hunting. But even tucked away, the tiny cubs were in danger.

Born just a few weeks before, they weighed less than two pounds each. They couldn't see clearly. Threats were everywhere. In the sky, eagles soared, ready to grab the cubs with their sharp talons. On the ground, king cobras and mamba snakes slithered through the tall, golden grass, ready to bite with their deadly venom. At night, hyenas and jackals hunted in hungry packs.

And most fearsome of all: lions. In this part of Africa, powerful lions truly are kings.

A mother cheetah with her cubs in the grasslands of Kenya.

The cubs slept while their mother roamed the scrubby land in search of prey. Hours went by. When the cubs awakened, they sniffed for their mother. They cried out. Their tiny stomachs ached with hunger. Strange sounds echoed around them—the hoots of baboons, the shrieks of hyenas.

Maybe they heard the roar of the lion that attacked their mother. Their mother probably

fought back, desperate to return to her cubs. But she would have been weak from recently giving birth. And cheetahs—light and slender—are built for speed, not strength. No creature on Earth can run faster. But in a fight, she was no match for hulking lions, with their massive muscles, iron-grip jaws, and tearing teeth.

Likely, the cheetah mother died very quickly, leaving her helpless cubs behind.

LUCKY CUBS

Even with a mother's protection, life is dangerous for cheetah cubs. Approximately 95 percent of all wild cheetah cubs die before they are three months old. Many die of diseases common to cheetahs.

Others are carried away by lions, vultures, and other predators. This is one reason why cheetahs are endangered. Today there are only about 7,100 of these big cats left in the wild. Most live in Africa.

But these cheetah cubs—both male—were lucky. Within a few days of their mother's death, two young boys—members of the Samburu tribe—heard their desperate cries.

The boys rescued the cubs and brought them to a couple named Jane and Ian Craig. For years, the Craigs had been working to help cheetahs and other endangered animals. They are the founders of an organization called the Lewa [LAY-wuh] Wildlife Conservancy. Lewa has turned 100 square miles of Kenyan wilderness into a wildlife refuge—a safe space for animals.

Inside the electrified fence of the refuge, animals are protected from human threats. Hunting and farming are banned. Visitors are strictly limited. An armed security force protects animals from poachers—hunters who kill endangered animals,

CHEETAH FACT Until 10,000 years ago, cheetahs also lived in North America.

often to sell their horns, skins, or other body parts.

When the two boys arrived with the cheetah cubs, the Craigs and their team snapped into action. The little cats were on the brink of death—starving, thirsty, and terrified. Over the next few weeks, the cubs received 24-hour-a-day attention.

Staffers cradled them like infants, fed them with bottles, slept with them, and comforted them. And they named them: Sambu and Toki. Within a few weeks, the cubs were scampering around their enclosure like frisky kittens.

But what next? What would become of these orphans?

The Lewa team felt it was urgent to get the cubs into the wilderness, where they could find mates. The vast protected grasslands of Lewa would make an ideal home for the cheetahs. The area is filled with gazelles and antelopes, which are favorite cheetah prey.

THE SAMBURU PEOPLE
OF NORTHERN KENYA

People in Kenya belong to many different tribes. The boys who found the cheetah cubs are members of the Samburu tribe.

A Samburu woman at a protest to protect endangered animals.

GLOBAL MARCH

In recent years, members of the Samburu tribe have worked closely with conservationists who protect their lands and the creatures that live there.

The northern
Kenyan wilderness

But how would the cheetahs survive on their own? In the wild, cubs stay with their mothers until they are almost two years old. During that time, cheetah mothers painstakingly teach their young how to hunt, how to avoid danger, and how to protect themselves. On Lewa's land, animals are safe from humans—but not from one another. The whole idea is to enable animals to live in their own natural habitat. For cheetahs, this means a world of dangers.

The cubs had much to learn about living in the wild. But who would teach them? The Craigs

Simon King
in action.

wouldn't be able to find a cheetah mother to school the cubs in the ways of the wild. So they settled for the next best thing: a man named Simon King.

WILD LESSONS

King is a Kenya-born award-winning wildlife filmmaker who had spent years studying cheetahs and other animals. His film work had already connected him to Lewa and its mission.

And his years of studying cheetahs had given him detailed knowledge of their behavior. Taking care of two baby cubs would be a huge time commitment for Simon. For two years, he would have to spend most of his time with them at his side. But he felt there was no other choice. And so, when the brothers were one month old, Simon became their father.

Simon quickly fell under the spell of the brothers. And they became attached to Simon—following him everywhere, nuzzling him with their triangular faces, twisting their elastic bodies around his legs whenever he came near.

Before long, Simon was taking the cubs on excursions into the more remote areas of Lewa. He worked closely with Stephen Yiasoi Saipan, a member of the local Maasai tribe.

If they saw large animals that posed a danger—black rhinos, lions, baboons—Simon or Stephen would growl at the cubs like a mother cheetah would, signaling to them to stay away. They learned quickly.

STALKING PREY

Hunting was a more difficult skill to teach. In the wild, a male cheetah must hunt successfully about twice a week to stay healthy. Often a mother cheetah will bring a live impala fawn back to her cubs to practice on. This was not something that

Simon won the trust of the cheetah cubs and became their devoted teacher.

Simon was willing—or able—to do. So he had to figure out some creative ideas for hunting lessons.

One afternoon, he showed the cheetahs a toy rabbit tied to a string. The brothers hissed at the creature. "What is that?" they seemed to say. "How do we know it won't attack us?" In response, Simon rolled around on the lawn with the stuffed rabbit, "proving" that it wasn't a threat. Soon, the cubs were tackling the rabbit and chasing after it as Simon pulled it around on its string. The

SAFE IN THE WILD

At Lewa, cheetahs and other endangered species are protected from human-made threats.

BLACK RHINO

GREVY'S ZEBRA

AFRICAN ELEPHANT

WILD DOG

hunting lessons continued, and the brothers began to stalk prey on their own.

Progress was slow. At first, every chase ended in failure. The cubs didn't understand they were still too small and clumsy to be chasing full-grown animals. One kick of a zebra's hind legs can crush a cheetah's skull. But the brothers' skills improved, and they started aiming for smaller and weaker animals that they could easily overpower.

The brothers stalked as a team. But their bond went beyond the hunt. They "talked" to each other with short, high-pitched chirps. They snuggled together when they slept. One day, Sambu froze in fear trying to cross a river for the first time (cheetahs hate water). Toki went back and forth across it, as if to say, "Look! It's easy." Finally, Sambu made the leap right behind his brother.

TRAGEDY AND HEARTBREAK

As they approached the age of two, Simon knew the time had come for the brothers to live independently on Lewa. Radio-transmitting collars would enable Simon to track the cheetahs' whereabouts, but they would be on their own. At first, the transition went smoothly.

And then one night, disaster struck.

Sambu before the tragic night.

The brothers were asleep on some rocks when lions attacked. Toki escaped. Sambu didn't. For Simon, Sambu's death was a heartbreak that would last for years.

For Toki, it was a catastrophe. Life is hard enough for cheetahs in the wild. A lone male has a particularly difficult time. The two brothers had forged a bond not only of brotherhood: Together they would have been a hunting team. They would have looked out for each other.

Now Toki would be on his own.

And sure enough, not long after Sambu's death, Toki was attacked by a gang of three male cheetahs

Simon
and Toki

protecting their territory—his throat was slashed, and his hind legs were badly mauled. He recovered only because he had around-the-clock care at Lewa.

Simon and the Craigs wondered whether Toki could continue to live in the wild at Lewa. Those three male cheetahs were lurking; they would surely attack again.

HOME AT LAST

Finally, Simon and the team decided that Toki should be moved to a nearby refuge, which had fewer cheetahs than Lewa. Within that 90,000-acre refuge, protected by an electric fence, there was

a 1,700-acre area where Toki was free to roam. It wasn't a vast wilderness, but he could live independently, hunting on his own and, hopefully, finding a mate.

Simon and Toki made the trip together; Toki was given medicine so he would sleep through the airplane ride. But from the moment he woke up, he seemed pleased to be in this new place.

He walked confidently, marking his territory, something he had never done at Lewa. "This is home," he seemed to say.

Simon smiled.

A proud father indeed.

THE CHEETAH FILES

Turn the page to learn more about cheetahs and other big cats.

IF YOU WERE A CHEETAH . . .

You would live in the grasslands of Africa. A few of you would live in Iran.

Your spotted coat would blend in with the grassland, hiding you from predators and your prey.

You would need lots of rest. After a hunt, you'd need at least half an hour to catch your breath.

You wouldn't have to drink much water. You could go 3 to 4 days without a sip.

You would live to about 12 years old in the wild. But only 5 percent of cheetahs survive past the age of 3 months.

You wouldn't roar. You'd purr.

Purrrrrrrr

You could hunt during the day, unlike most other cats, which are nocturnal.

You would eat gazelles, antelopes, impalas, and small animals and birds.

A cheetah's coat blends in with the grass so I can't see it when it's stalking me!

SPEED

EYES can constantly refocus as the cheetah moves at high speed.

HEAD is small and compact, providing little resistance to the wind.

NOSTRILS are extra big for sucking in air.

HEART is bigger than hearts of other big cats, so it can pump more blood to muscles.

LUNGS are supersized to bring more oxygen to the heart and muscles.

Cheetahs are the fastest animal on land, able to rocket from zero to 70 miles an hour in three seconds. That's quicker than any other animal—or many sports cars.
How do they do it?

SPINE is flexible so back legs can come all the way forward during sprints.

TAIL is long and thin, for steering and for balance on quick turns.

CLAWS are always out and grip the ground like cleats.

The limits of speed
Cheetahs can sprint for only about 30 seconds, enough time to (hopefully) catch a gazelle or impala, knock it down, and kill it with a strong bite to its neck. But after making a kill, the cheetah is so exhausted from this 30-second rush that it must rest before eating.

THE WORLD OF

BIG CATS

Cheetahs are one of seven "big cats." All share some impressive traits. But each has its own unique powers.

I am a distant relative of big cats, but don't have much in common with them!

THE BIGGEST

I can devour more than 80 pounds of meat in one meal.

No two tigers have the same stripes—and they even have stripes on their skin.

Tigers are huge—a typical male can weigh 450 pounds—and are even stronger than lions. But lions and tigers never meet in the wild anymore. Most lions live in Africa, while wild tigers are found in India, Nepal, Bhutan, Russia, China, and other Asian countries.

Tigers live mostly alone, though cubs stay with their mothers until they are two.

You can hear my loud **ROAR** from 5 miles away.

MOST SOCIAL

Lions live together in groups called prides with as many as 30 other lions. Females hunt, while males defend territory.

Lions once lived all over Africa, Asia, and Europe. But today almost all are in Africa, where their numbers are shrinking.

Only males have manes; the darker the mane, the older the lion.

Cheetahs are fierce hunters in the wild, but show little aggression toward humans. That's why it was once common for wealthy people to keep cheetahs as pets or hunting companions.

Cheetahs were once kept as hunting companions. This photo is from 1907, in India.

This is cruel—no wild animal should be kept as a pet. Though keeping cheetahs as pets is illegal in most countries, thousands are still kept in private homes.

MOST MYSTERIOUS

Snow leopards live in mountains across Asia and Russia. Scientists don't know much about these animals in the wild because they're so hard to track in their rugged habitats.

> When I'm cold, I wrap my long, fluffy tail around myself for extra warmth.

MOST NAMES

Cougars are also known as panthers, pumas, mountain lions, and catamounts. They once roamed all across the United States. Today, almost all live in the far western states, where they feed on deer and other animals.

I'm the only big cat that lives in the wilds of the United States.

Jaguars are native to South and Central America, where they live mostly in rain forests and wetlands. They are powerful, and third in size behind tigers and lions.

But it's the jaguar's bite that is most impressive. A jaguar's jaw is strong enough to chomp through the shells

of turtles, the skin of crocodiles, and the skulls of other prey.

To the Aztec and Mayan peoples, the jaguar is a symbol of strength and courage.

138

Leopards can—and do—live in almost any kind of environment. They can be found in deserts, rain forests, swamps, or mountains. And they live all over the globe. But they are mostly found in Africa; populations in most other areas are endangered. They will also eat almost any kind of any animal, even snakes.

Cheetahs and jaguars have spots that are different from mine. Can you "spot" the difference?

WHICH IS WHICH?

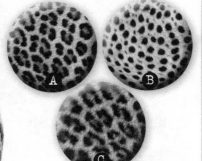

BIG CATS
IN DANGER

All seven kinds of big cats face serious threats in the wild. Most are in danger of disappearing from their habitats. Here's why.

❶ They are losing their lands

Every year, millions of acres of forests and other wild lands are being turned into ranches and farms. This is an especially big problem for big cats, which need a large area of land for hunting and breeding.

A logger cuts down trees in the Amazon rain forest in Brazil.

Weapons taken from a poacher who was hunting animals in the protected Amazon rain forest.

❷ They are hunted and sold

Cheetah cubs are captured from the wild to be sold as pets. Tigers, lions, and other big cats are killed for their skins and bones, which are ground up and sold to people who believe they prevent illness.

❸ They are killed as pests

As big cats lose their habitats, they are more likely to wander into towns, to kill farm animals, or to threaten humans. This leads to many big cats being killed.

PROTECTING BIG CATS

Here's how people are trying to help big cats.

Scientists with the National Park Service tend to a mountain lion in the California mountains.

SCIENTISTS are studying big cat diseases, and trying to make them healthier in the wild.

WARRIORS from native tribes like the Samburu are protecting lions and other animals on their lands.

Thandiwe Mweetwa works to protect big cats in the African country of Zambia, through the Zambian Carnivore Programme.

EDUCATORS are teaching about the benefits of protecting big cats in the wild.

ZT-TBV

For decades, filmmakers Beverly and Dereck Joubert's films have been helping in the fight to protect wilderness areas.

PHOTOGRAPHERS AND FILMMAKERS are sharing the beauty and magic of big cats—and their struggles—with the world.

TECHNOLOGY like drones help park rangers in Africa watch for poachers and other threats.

WILDLIFE REFUGES like Lewa provide large wilderness areas where big cats can live without human threats.

Turn the page to learn how YOU can help.

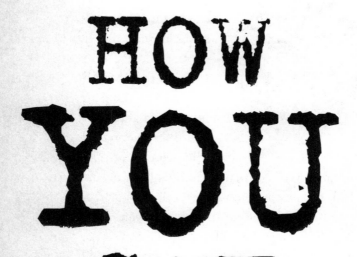

HOW YOU CAN HELP

Kids around the world are joining the mission to protect animals and our natural world.

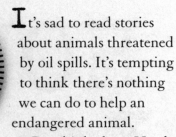

KIDS TAKING ACTION

It's sad to read stories about animals threatened by oil spills. It's tempting to think there's nothing we can do to help an endangered animal.

But think about Hardy Jones, who dedicated his life to helping sea mammals. Think about the Samburu kids of Kenya, who rescued the orphaned cheetahs and brought them to Lewa. Think about those hundreds of people who rushed to saved penguins after the oil spill. Think about what would happen if everyone rallied to protect the incredible animals we share our world with.

HERE'S WHAT YOU CAN DO.

EXPLORE
Learn all you can about animals and their wild places. The more you know, the more inspired you will be.

SPEAK OUT
Tell your friends and family what you've learned about animals and how we can protect the environment. Show support for causes you believe in.

CLEAN UP Be respectful when you are outdoors. Volunteer to clean a beach, a trail, a city park. The animals will thank you!

Thank you!

Turn the page for great books and other resources!

 **Read more about World War I and animals that helped humans.**

NONFICTION

STUBBY THE WAR DOG
by Ann Bausum, National Geographic Kids, 2018

THE WAR TO END ALL WARS: WORLD WAR I
by Russell Freedman, Clarion Books, 2013

NATIONAL GEOGRAPHIC KIDS: EVERYTHING WORLD WAR I
by Karen Kenney, National Geographic Kids, 2014

TREATIES, TRENCHES, MUD, AND BLOOD: (NATHAN HALE'S HAZARDOUS TALES #4)
by Nathan Hale, Amulet Books, 2014

FICTION

WAR HORSE
by Michael Morpurgo, Scholastic Press, 2010

PAX
by Sarah Pennypacker, Balzer + Bray, 2019

I'm way more fascinating than most people know!

Dive deeper for more information about sea mammals and oceans.

NONFICTION

TRACKING TRASH
by Loree Griffin Burns, HMH Books for Kids, 2018

EIGHT DOLPHINS OF KATRINA: A TRUE TALE OF SURVIVAL
by Janet Wyman Coleman, Houghton Mifflin Harcourt, 2017

NATIONAL GEOGRAPHIC KIDS: DOLPHINS
by Melissa Stewart, National Geographic Kids, 2010

WINTER'S TAIL
by Craig Hatkoff, Scholastic Press, 2009

FICTION

DOLPHIN DREAMS
by Catherine Hapka, Scholastic Press, 2017

HOW TO SPEAK DOLPHIN
by Ginny Rorby, Scholastic Press, 2017

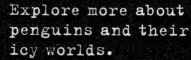

Explore more about penguins and their icy worlds.

NONFICTION

ALL ABOUT PENGUINS
by Dyan deNapoli, Rockridge Press, 2020

OIL SPILL!: DISASTER IN THE GULF OF MEXICO
by Elaine Landau, Millbrook Press, 2011

THE GREAT PENGUIN RESCUE
by Sandra Markle, Millbrook Press, 2017, 2009

FICTION

MR. POPPER'S PENGUINS
by Florence and Richard Atwater, Little, Brown and Company, 1938

There's so much more to learn about me!

 Hunt for more facts about cheetahs and other big cats.

NONFICTION

CHASING CHEETAHS: THE RACE TO SAVE AFRICA'S FASTEST CATS
by Sy Montgomery, HMH Books, 2014

HOW IT WAS WITH DOOMS
by Xan and Carol Hopcraft, Aladdin, 2000

NATIONAL GEOGRAPHIC KIDS: EVERYTHING BIG CATS
by Elizabeth Carney, National Geographic Kids, 2011

FICTION

WHEN YOU TRAP A TIGER
by Tae Keller, Random House, 2020

JOIN THEIR MISSION

These six organizations are working to save animals and our planet. Explore their websites and support their work.

1 World Wildlife Fund

Discover all you need to know about endangered animals and how you can help them survive in the wild.
worldwildlife.org

2 Rainforest Trust

Explore the world's rain forests and how you can help protect them.
rainforesttrust.org

3 Natural Resources Defense Council

Learn how you can help protect Earth's resources and fight climate change.
nrdc.org

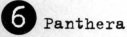 **Cheetah Conservation Fund**

Join scientists and researchers in the race to save cheetahs in the wild.

cheetah.org

5 **Ocean Conservancy**

Support the fight to keep our oceans healthy for all creatures.

oceanconservancy.org

6 **Panthera**

Help support the mission to protect big cats around the world.

panthera.org

KNOW BEFORE YOU GIVE

Check out Charity Navigator.
This organization rates charities based
on how much of each donation really
goes to help the cause.

charitynavigator.org

ACKNOWLEDGMENTS

I want to thank my *Storyworks* family—Rebecca Leon, Kristin Lewis, Allison Friedman, Albert Amigo, Lois Safrani, Alison Colby, and Bianca Alexis. Being a part of this team brings me more joy and inspiration than I can express.

I also want to thank my wonderful editor Katie Woehr for her laser focus, vision, and no-detail-too-small support of all things I Survived. Huge thanks and love to the entire I Survived team: Heather Daugherty, Katie Fitch, Debra Dorfman, Erin Berger, Meaghan Finnerty, and Alex Kelleher-Negorski.

And this book would not have come to life without designer Deb Dinger, my friend, creative partner and *Storyworks* sister of more than two decades, who brought her usual love, care, and creative brilliance to every page.

Finally, to all of my *Storyworks* and I Survived teachers, families and readers, thank you for giving my work meaning and purpose, and for making my stories a part of your lives.

ABOUT THE AUTHOR

LAUREN TARSHIS'S *New York Times* bestselling I Survived series tells stories of young people and their resilience and strength in the midst of unimaginable disasters and times of turmoil. Lauren has brought her signature warmth, integrity, and exhaustive research to topics such as the September 11 attacks, the American Revolution, Hurricane Katrina, the bombing of Pearl Harbor, and other world events. In addition to being the editor-in-chief and publisher of Scholastic's Classroom Magazines, Lauren is the longtime editorial director of *Storyworks* Magazine. Lauren is also the author of the critically acclaimed novels *Emma-Jean Lazarus Fell Out of a Tree* and *Emma-Jean Lazarus Fell in Love*, and the picture book *Only My Dog Knows I Pick My Nose*. Lauren lives in Connecticut with her family, and can be found online at **Laurentarshis.com**.

PHOTO CREDITS

BIBLIOGRAPHY

Here are some key resources I used
to write these articles.

PIGEONS
A FEATHERED RIVER ACROSS THE SKY: THE PASSENGER
PIGEON'S FLIGHT TO EXTINCTION, *by Joel Greenberg,
Bloomsbury, 2014*

OPERATION COLUMBIA: THE SECRET PIGEON SERVICE OF
WORLD WAR II, *by Gordon Corera, William Morrow, 2018*

THE HOMING PIGEON, *by George E. Howard, 1901, reprinted in 2017*

DOLPHINS
THE VOICE OF THE DOLPHINS, *by Hardy Jones, Imagewrite, 2011*

SECRETS OF THE WHALES, *by Brian Skerry, National Geographic, 2021*

INTERVIEW WITH HARDY JONES, PBS.COM, 2008

PENGUINS
EVERY PENGUIN IN THE WORLD, A QUEST TO SEE THEM
ALL, *by Charles Bergman, Sasquatch Books, 2020*

THE GREAT PENGUIN RESCUE, 40,000 PENGUINS, A
DEVASTATING OIL SPILL, AND THE INSPIRING STORY OF
THE WORLD'S LARGEST ANIMAL RESCUE, *by Dyan deNapoli,
Free Press, 2010*

THE CONTINENT OF ANTARCTICA, *by Julian Dowdeswell and
Michael Hambrey, Papadakis, 2019*

CHEETAHS
INTERVIEW WITH SIMON KING, *June 23, 2010, PBS.org*

REMEMBERING LIONS, *by Margo Raggett, Remembering Wildlife, 2020*

THE CRY OF THE KALAHARI, *by Mark and Delia Owens, Mariner
Books, 1992*

"CHEETAHS ARE PERILOUSLY CLOSE TO EXTINCTION,"
by Alexandra Petri, National Geographic, December 27, 2016

When disaster strikes, heroes are made.

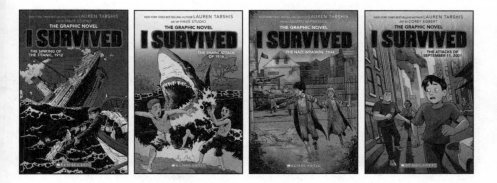

REAL KIDS.
REAL DISASTERS.

I Survived True Stories feature riveting narrative non-fiction stories of unimaginable destruction—and, against all odds, survival.

scholastic.com/isurvived